A LOOK AROUND SPACE

Willowisp Press

by Margaret Holland, Ph.D.
and David Cooper
illustrated by Thomas O. Miller

Published by Willowisp Press, Inc.
401 E. Wilson Bridge Road, Worthington, Ohio 43085

Printed in the United States of America

10 9 8 7 6 5 4 3 2 1

ISBN 0-87406-037-0

Photograph of the moon on page 13 by Dale Briggs. All other photographs and the artist's drawings on pages 23 and 31 were provided courtesy of the National Aeronautics and Space Administration (NASA).

Special thanks to William K. Hartmann, Ph.D., Senior Astronomer, Planetary Science Institute, Tucson, Arizona; Ray Villard, Producer, Davis Planetarium, Maryland Academy of Sciences; Ron Miller, former Art Director, Albert Einstein Spacearium, National Air and Space Museum, Smithsonian Institution; and the Public Information Offices of NASA Johnson Space Center, Houston, Texas, and NASA Jet Propulsion Laboratory, Pasadena, California.

We humans live on the earth. And our planet earth is surrounded by space. The sky is what we see of space. There are billions of stars and probably billions of other planets moving through space. Our planet is moving through space, too.

We live on the surface of our planet earth. Gravity keeps us here on the earth. Gravity is an invisible force that pulls things and people toward the center of the earth. All the other planets and stars and moons have gravity, too. Without gravity we would float away into space.

GRAVITY

NO GRAVITY

We human beings have always wanted to know what is out in space. We have created telescopes and spaceships to find out. Astronomers use giant telescopes to study the moon and stars and planets. Astronauts travel in spaceships to explore space. Robot spaceships explore parts of space that are too far away for people to visit.

This picture of the planet earth was taken from a spaceship. The earth looks mostly blue and white. The blue is water. The earth is mostly covered by water. The land covers less than a third of the earth. The white in the photograph shows clouds that cover the earth.

Small robot spaceships called satellites send important information back to the earth.

Weather satellites send pictures that show where storms are located. You can see these pictures on TV weather forecasts.

Our planet earth is moving through space. It is traveling in a giant loop around the sun. The earth takes a year—365 days—to go around the sun. The earth is also spinning like a merry-go-round. It turns one complete turn in each 24-hour day.

The sun lights up the earth. The earth turns around each day. The half of the earth turned away from the sun is dark. On that half of the earth it is night. The half of the earth turned toward the sun is light. On that half it is daytime.

Spaceships can fly around the earth in one and a half hours. They fly around the earth in about as much time as it takes you to get up and get dressed and go to school each morning.

The moon is our nearest neighbor in space. The moon is smaller than the earth. It moves around the earth in a path called an orbit. Our astronauts have visited the moon. A spaceship takes two and a half days to go from the earth to the moon.

So far only twelve people from the earth have actually landed on the moon. The first human beings to walk on the moon were astronauts Neil Armstrong and "Buzz" Aldrin. They put a piece of metal on the moon that says: "Here men from the planet earth first set foot upon the moon. . . . We came in peace for all mankind."

The astronauts used the lunar rover to explore the moon. They found that the moon has no air or water. The moon is covered with rocks and powdery dust. It has mountains and craters. Craters are hollow places that look like the inside of a bowl.

Because there is no air or water, nothing grows on the moon. No grass or trees or animals can live there. Days on the moon are much hotter than on the earth. Nights on the moon are much colder.

The moon seen from the earth.

Like the earth, the moon is lit by the sun. When you look at the moon from the earth, you sometimes see a full moon, one complete side of the moon. Other times you see a half moon or crescent moon. How much of the moon you see depends on where the moon is in its orbit around the earth.

Astronauts on the moon saw the earth the same way. Sometimes they could see "full" earth, other times "half" earth or "crescent" earth.

The earth seen from the moon.

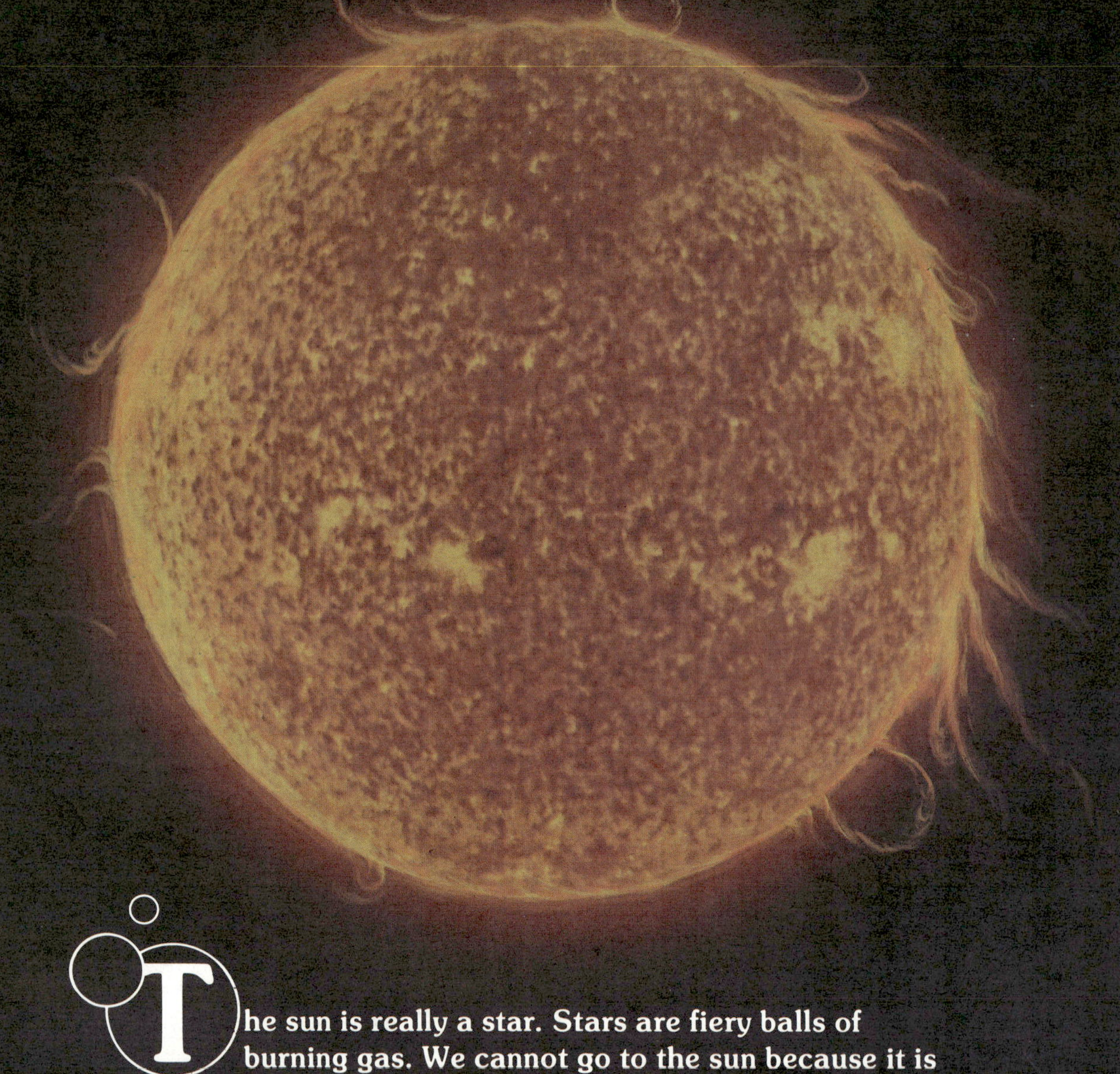

The sun is really a star. Stars are fiery balls of burning gas. We cannot go to the sun because it is much too hot. If our robot spaceships were sent to the sun, they would burn up long before they got there.

Venus is the second planet from the sun. It is the closest planet to the earth and about the same size as the earth. Venus is so hot, no earthlike plants or animals can live there.

You can easily see Venus in the sky without a telescope. But even the strongest telescopes cannot see the surface. Venus is always covered by thick clouds. These clouds are made of acid instead of water. The robot spaceships that went to Venus could not take clear photographs through the thick clouds.

Mars is the next planet beyond the earth away from the sun. Mars is about half as big as the earth. You can see Mars in the sky without a telescope. Our telescopes show that Mars has two ice caps at its poles, just as the earth does. And it has two moons.

Robot spaceships landed on Mars. Pictures were sent back by the spaceships. These pictures showed that the surface of Mars looks very much like deserts on the earth. But the dirt is red and the sky is pink.

For many years people have imagined that there are intelligent humanlike beings on Mars. But there is no breathable air on Mars. So earthlike beings could not live there.

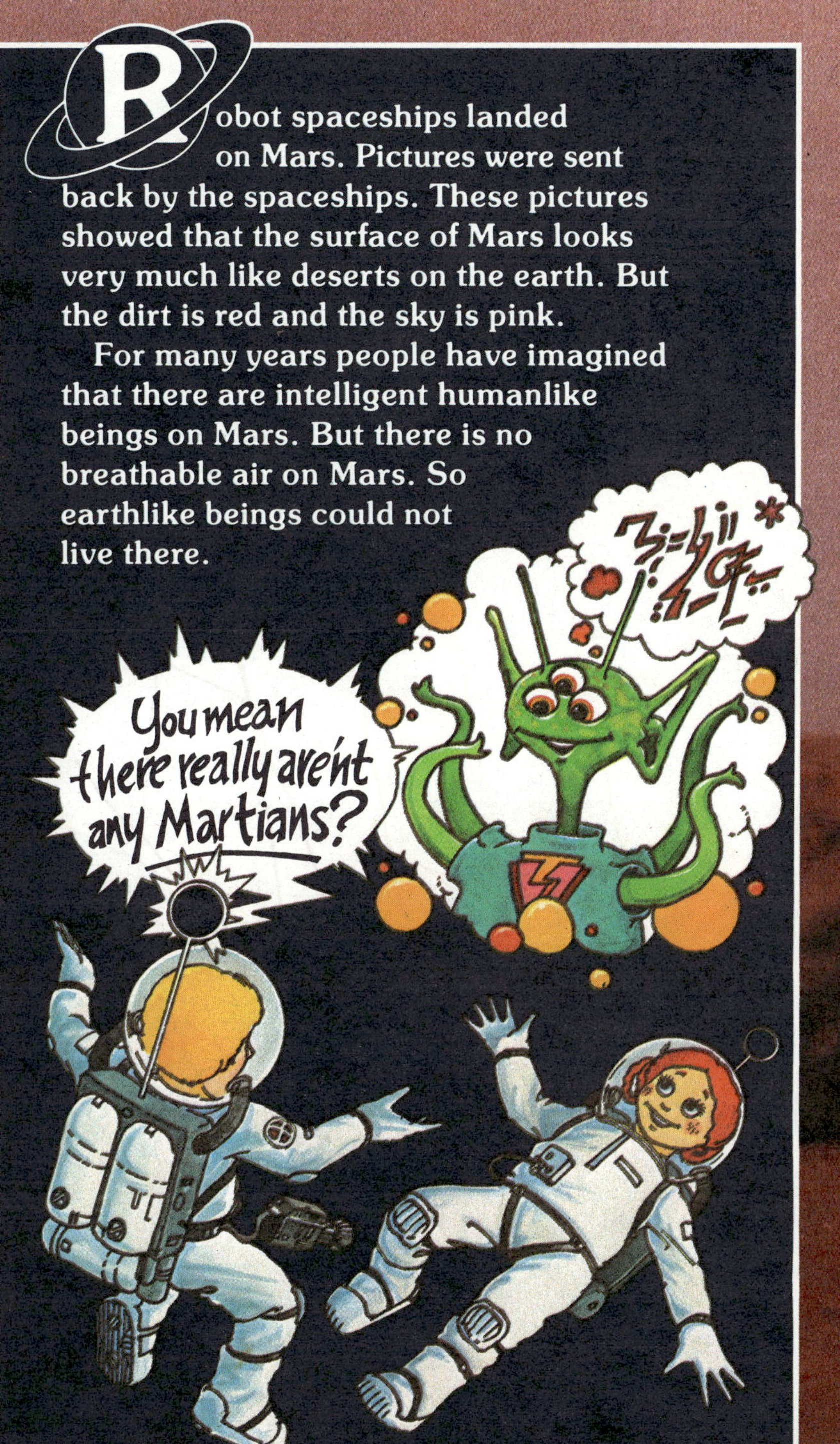

Jupiter is the biggest planet in our solar system. Robot spaceships have gone past Jupiter and sent back pictures of gas clouds. Jupiter may have a liquid surface beneath thick clouds.

Saturn is the second largest planet. It has hundreds of rings around it. The rings are made of millions of icy particles. Saturn has at least twenty moons.

The three planets farthest from the earth are Uranus, Neptune, and tiny Pluto. Right now robot spaceships from the earth are traveling past Uranus and on toward Neptune. These spaceships have been traveling since 1977. The spaceships will send back new information about these two planets.

Comets are small chunks of frozen gases traveling in space. When they enter our solar system, they go into orbit around the sun.

Halley's Comet is the most famous of all comets. It can be seen for several months every 76 years. That means most people see it only once during their lifetimes.

Have you ever seen a bright streak go across the sky at night? These streaks are called meteors or shooting stars. Meteors are small solid objects that burn up when they enter the air high above the earth.

Our solar system—the sun and its nine known planets—is a very tiny part of space. The sun is just a medium-sized star. Billions of stars may have planets revolving around them. The solar system is a very small part of the Milky Way galaxy. This one galaxy may contain as many as 200,000,000,000 (200 billion) stars.

WE ARE HERE!

There are many, many galaxies. The nearest major galaxy to the Milky Way is Andromeda. Astronomers use giant telescopes to study this great spiral galaxy.

There are probably millions of earthlike planets among the galaxies. Many astronomers think there are very likely other beings, much like human beings, out there somewhere in space.

We can travel in the part of space close to us. The new space shuttle helps us travel more easily. The space shuttle can take people and supplies to and from orbiting robot spaceships and our future space stations.

Powerful rocket boosters help launch the shuttle. Then the boosters drop off and parachute back to the earth.

The space shuttle can carry up to seven people on trips lasting as long as thirty days. Once the shuttle is in orbit, the crew can open the cargo doors and link with robot spaceships. When the shuttle comes back to the earth, it lands like a glider.

Inside the space shuttle there is no gravity. The astronauts float around, and their hair sticks out in all directions.

The astronauts wear space suits when they go outside the shuttle. They make repairs on robot spaceships and do experiments.

Future space stations will help us learn more about living and working in space. They will help us look and listen much better for messages from other parts of the universe.

No one knows what the future may bring. One day you may be able to live in space. You may actually make contact with beings from other parts of space. There is no end to what can be learned about space.

INDEX